# Arts and Crafts
## of
# ANCIENT GREECE

## Ting Morris
### Illustrated by Emma Young

A⁺
**Smart Apple Media**

Published by Smart Apple Media
2140 Howard Drive West, North Mankato, MN 56003

Artwork by Emma Young
Designed by Helen James
Edited by Mary-Jane Wilkins
Picture research by Su Alexander

Photograph acknowledgements
Front cover Gianni Dagli Orti/Corbis; page 5l Christie's Images/Corbis,
r Sandro Vannini/Corbis; 6 Archivo Iconografico,S.A./Corbis; 7 Copyright The Trustees
of The British Museum; 8 Gianni Dagli Orti/Corbis; 9 Mimmo Jodice/Corbis; 10
Bettmann/Corbis; 12 Vanni Archive/Corbis; 13t bpk/Antikensammlung, SMB/Juergen
Liepe, b Mimmo Jodice/Corbis; 14 & 15 Copyright The Trustees of The British Museum;
18 Charles O'Rear/Corbis; 19t Bettmann/Corbis, b Copyright The Trustees of The
British Museum; 20 Bettmann/Corbis; 21 Werner Forman/Corbis; 24 Gianni Dagli Orti/
Corbis; 25t Larry Lee photography/Corbis, b Bill Ross/Corbis; 27t David Forman;
Eye Ubiquitous/Corbis, b Massimo Listri/Corbis; 28 Erich Lessing/AKG Images

Printed in Singapore

Library of Congress Cataloging-in-Publication Data

Morris, Ting.
Ancient Greece / by Ting Morris.
p. cm. — (Arts and crafts of)
Includes index.
ISBN-13: 978-1-58340-912-1
1. Handicraft—Greece—History—Juvenile literature. 2. Clothing and dress—
History—Juvenile literature. 3. Greece—Civilization—Juvenile literature. I.
Title. II. Series.

TT75.M67 2006
680.938—dc22  2005056776

First Edition

9 8 7 6 5 4 3 2 1

# Contents

# The world of the ancient Greeks

In ancient times, many cultures and civilizations flourished on the mainland and islands that make up Greece. The Bronze Age started there about 5,000 years ago, and the first culture grew up around the Cyclades, a group of more than 200 islands in the Aegean Sea. Then came the Minoan civilization on the island of Crete, from about 2500 to 1200 B.C. After this, the mainland city of Mycenae became most important.

The land around the eastern region of the Mediterranean Sea made up the ancient Greek world. It included parts of Asia Minor, where Turkey is today.

Around 500 B.C., the period known as the Classical Age began in Greece. This was the golden age of Athens, a city that attracted the best scholars and artists of the time. They developed ideas about art and architecture that have influenced all of Western civilization. Their achievements still have an effect on us today.

## Early sculpture

The Cyclades islands were named after the Greek word *kyklos*, meaning "circle," because they formed a circle around the island of Delos. The islanders used bronze (mixed copper and tin) tools. Before this, they made marble figurines and smoothed their sculptures with pebbles of a hard rock called emery.

This marble figurine was made around 4500 B.C. She has a sculpted nose, and her eyes and mouth might originally have been painted on. Figures like this were placed in tombs, probably to protect the dead.

## The rise of Macedonia

Ancient Macedonia covered much of the northeastern region of the modern Greek mainland. By 338 B.C., a Macedonian king, Philip II, controlled Greece, and the golden age of Classical Athens had ended. Two years later, Philip's son became king. He built a great empire and became known as Alexander the Great. The arts flourished under Alexander. Historians call the next few centuries the Hellenistic (meaning "Greek") period.

This marble head of Alexander the Great dates from around 150 B.C. By this time, sculptors were making faces look lifelike. The head was found in Alexandria, the Egyptian city founded by Alexander and where his tomb was built.

# Metalworkers in gold and bronze

Gold and silver were precious metals to the ancient Greeks, just as they are to us today. Bronze was used mainly for larger items such as statues.

In Athens, metalworkers had their own quarter beside the *agora*, or marketplace. This craft district was next to the temple of Hephaistos, the Greek god of fire and metalwork. Legend says that he made the armor of Achilles. On the other side of the *agora* was the mint, where metal coins were made. Craftsmen produced the first Athenian coins in 575 B.C.

A gold death mask from Mycenae. It was made by heating a sheet of metal and hammering it into shape.

## Grave goods

In 1876, German archaeologist Heinrich Schliemann discovered six royal graves at the site of the ancient citadel of Mycenae. Nineteen people were buried there, including

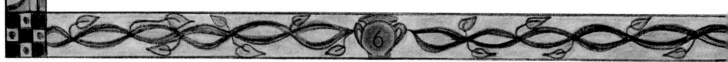

women and children, along with an amazing collection of gold objects. The faces of five kings were covered with gold masks, which experts think were portraits. There were also gold vessels, cups, and all kinds of jewelry. The people were buried around 1600 B.C., when the Mycenaeans were expert goldsmiths.

## Beating and casting bronze

At the beginning of the Bronze Age, the Greeks worked metals mainly by beating. Craftsmen heated flat sheets of bronze and hammered them into shape around a carved piece of wood. Later, they learned how to cast the molten metal inside a pottery mold. Some used the lost-wax method. In this process, a statue was first shaped in wax around a clay core. The wax was covered in another layer of clay and then heated. The wax melted and ran out, leaving a gap into which molten bronze could be poured. The bronze took the shape of the sculpted wax, and when the bronze was cool, the clay shape was removed.

This bronze figurine of a running girl was cast around 500 B.C. She may have been a runner at the Heraea, a festival similar to the Olympic Games held in honor of the goddess Hera.

# Greek painting

More than 3,000 years ago, artists decorated the palaces of Minoan Crete and Mycenae with fresco paintings. Wall-painting continued in later Greece, and some artists began painting on wooden panels. The wood was first coated with white paint, then bright colors were added.

Artists used a technique called encaustic painting. They mixed paints with hot wax, brushed this onto the wood, and then burned in the colors with a red-hot rod. The first great master of the Classical Age was Polygnotus, who worked in Athens around 450 B.C. He was followed by Pamphilos of Macedonia, who was an expert in the technique. Almost all ancient Greek paintings are lost, but Roman artists made many copies, and some of these still survive.

## Early murals

Frescoes similar to Cretan ones were painted on the walls of houses on the Cyclades islands. The most complete set of frescoes was found buried under volcanic ash in the town of Akrotiri, on the island of Santorini (known as Thera in ancient times). There was a huge volcanic explosion there around 1500 B.C.

This fresco shows children boxing. It was in one of the rooms excavated at Akrotiri. The children may have been brother and sister.

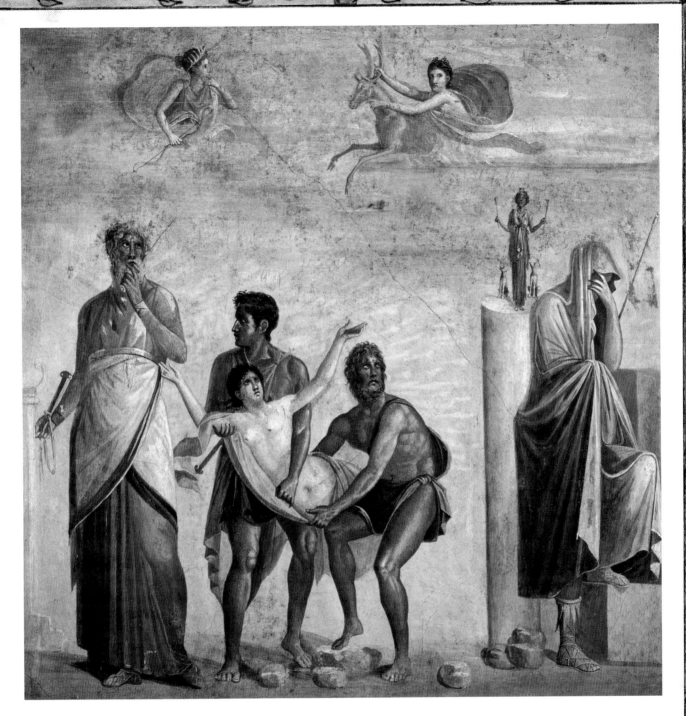

## Heroes and heroines

Roman copies of Greek wall paintings show that
Greek artists often based their wall paintings on myths
and legendary adventures. The 12 labors of Herakles
("Hercules" to the Romans) were a favorite theme.
Many copies of original Greek paintings were found
in the Roman city of Pompeii, which was destroyed
by a volcanic eruption in A.D. 79.

This wall painting is a Roman
copy of a painting by the
Greek artist Timanthes.
It shows the capture of
Iphigenia, daughter of the
Mycenaean king Agamemnon,
who is covering his face with
his cloak.

# Paint a mural

Minoan artists decorated the palace walls at Knossos with frescoes. They put on the first layer of paint when the plaster was wet, so the paint went into the surface and was set in the wall. They used mainly blue, which they mixed from a form of copper, yellow (from ochre), black (from carbon), white (from lime), and red (from a form of iron).

This beautiful fresco of dolphins and fish is on the wall of the queen's chamber at the Minoan Palace of Knossos.

## Paint a dolphin mural

You will need: a cardboard lid 6 by 7 by 1 inches (15 x 18 x 2.5 cm) deep • modeling clay • blue and white powder paint • brushes • a sponge • poster paint • plaster of Paris • fine sandpaper • masking tape • cardboard

**1** Build a wall. Use the lid as a mold, lined with a thin layer of clay. Mix the plaster of Paris with water to a creamy consistency. Add a little blue powder paint to make a sea background. Pour it into the mold and allow it to set for a few hours. (Never pour waste plaster down the sink!)

**2** When the plaster is dry, turn it out of the mold. Peel off the clay and smooth the surface with fine sandpaper. Mix poster paint into a light muddy sea color and stipple it onto the wall with a sponge. Sprinkle white powder paint on the wet surface and overpaint it with a wide brush to create a wavy background. Allow to dry.

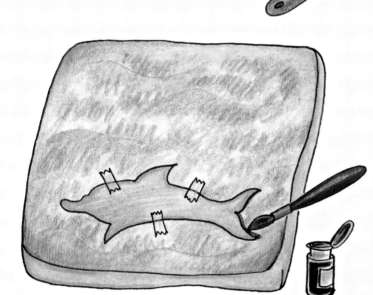

**3** Copy the dolphin outline onto cardboard. Make it big enough to cover half the wall. Cut it out. Tape the shape onto the wall with masking tape while you draw around it with a fine brush. Then turn the cut-out over so the second dolphin swims the other way. Draw around the shape as before. Color the dolphins with poster paints.

**4** Paint two stripes at the bottom of the picture and copy the pattern of the border to show that your picture is a mural.

# Archaic sculpture

The Greeks started making large statues of their gods and other subjects at the start of the Archaic Period, around 700 B.C. Early Greek sculptors were inspired by the Egyptian tradition and copied some of its features. Many early Greek figures stood stiffly, with arms close to their sides and often with the left foot forward.

The female figure was called *kore* (or "maiden"), and she wore draped clothing. The Greeks usually painted the stone sculptures with red hair and lips and black eyebrows and lashes. The male figure, called *kouros* ("youth"), was usually naked. Both male and female figures had elaborate hairstyles. After about 550 B.C., new techniques of hollow casting allowed sculptors to make large statues in bronze, and this soon became the most popular material for sculpure.

## Ancient smile

Archaic Greek statues usually had oval or triangular faces. Most had a strange, gentle smile. Perhaps this was meant to make the face look pleasant.

This marble sculpture dates from about 560 B.C. and is probably the oldest surviving equestrian statue. The horseman has an archaic smile, and the wreath on his head suggests that he has won one of the Greek games.

This Archaic maiden has a braided hairstyle that was often shown on this kind of sculpture.

The Archaic style is often called Daedalic, after a legendary Athenian sculptor and inventor named Daedalus. He is most famous for making wings for himself and his son Icarus so they could fly.

## Tomb guardian

Archaic sculptures were usually people, but some were animals. Horses and lions were common subjects. They were often placed at the entrance to tombs as the symbolic guardians of the dead. The few sculptures that survive show that by the sixth century B.C. Greek artists were no longer copying the style of others.

This marble lion dates from about 525 B.C., and was found guarding a tomb at the port of Miletus on the coast of Asia Minor (modern Turkey).

# Black and red pottery

Greeks began to use the potter's wheel more than 4,000 years ago. The craft of pottery flourished from then on and became one of the most important art forms of ancient Greece.

Vases were made in many different styles and decorated in a variety of ways. The most famous were Attic vases from Athens. Around 500 people worked in a pottery district called the Keramaikos. Athenian potters moved on from early geometric patterns to make black-figure pottery starting around 600 B.C. Around 530 B.C., there was a big change when the black figures on the pots turned to red.

## Firing black figures

To make a vase, potters turned a lump of clay on a wheel and shaped it by hand. In the Keramaikos district, the wheel was usually turned by hand by a young male apprentice.

This black-figure dinos (or bowl) and stand were made in Athens around 580 B.C. The bowl shows a wedding procession and is signed "Sophilos painted me." This is the earliest Greek vase-painter known.

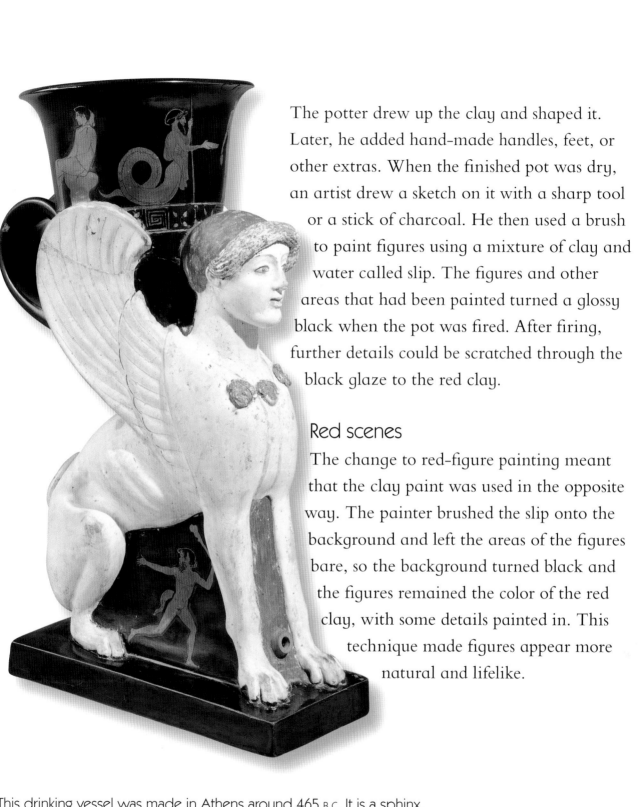

The potter drew up the clay and shaped it. Later, he added hand-made handles, feet, or other extras. When the finished pot was dry, an artist drew a sketch on it with a sharp tool or a stick of charcoal. He then used a brush to paint figures using a mixture of clay and water called slip. The figures and other areas that had been painted turned a glossy black when the pot was fired. After firing, further details could be scratched through the black glaze to the red clay.

## Red scenes

The change to red-figure painting meant that the clay paint was used in the opposite way. The painter brushed the slip onto the background and left the areas of the figures bare, so the background turned black and the figures remained the color of the red clay, with some details painted in. This technique made figures appear more natural and lifelike.

This drinking vessel was made in Athens around 465 B.C. It is a sphinx, and the cup has red-figure scenes. When the Greeks poured wine into the cup, they covered the spout at the bottom with a finger. The finger was removed to pour the wine into a shallow drinking cup.

# Make an amphora

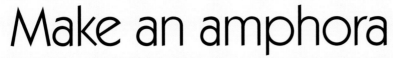

Greek pots were made in various shapes and sizes. An amphora was a large storage jar for wine, olive oil, honey, and other liquids. It was about 18 inches (45 cm) tall, with two sturdy handles for lifting and a wide, round bottom. The handles and bottom were made separately and then attached to the amphora.

From left to right: kylix (drinking cup), amphora, hydria (water jar), krater (for mixing wine with water), lekythos (flask for olive oil).

## Make your own amphora

You will need: air-hardening clay • white, ready-mixed paint • poster paints • brushes • a sponge • polyurethane varnish • a modeling tool • white vinegar

**1** To make the bowl, knead a ball of clay in your hands until it is soft and smooth. Hold it in one hand and push the thumb of your other hand into the clay to make a hole. Turn the ball and pinch out the sides with your thumb and finger until it forms a bowl. Keep the rim fat.

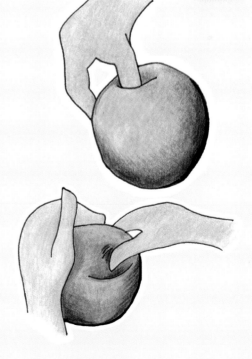

**2** To make the bottom, set the bowl upside down. Roll a lump of clay into a thick coil. Use a modeling tool to make criss-cross marks and score a circle on the bottom of the bowl. Moisten the scored circle with a little vinegar and water, and press the coil onto it. Seal the joint by smearing it over with your finger. Allow to firm up, then stand the pot on the bottom.

**3** Build up the neck with thick clay coils. Roll out coils of the same thickness and add one on top of another. Score and moisten the tops as you go, placing ring upon ring, always smearing the inside of the coil down onto the one below. To make the neck slope outward, place a coil toward the outside edge of the one underneath.

**4** Roll out two thick coils for handles. Score each side of the vase just below the rim and a little lower. Moisten with vinegar and water, and press the coils into place. Allow to dry.

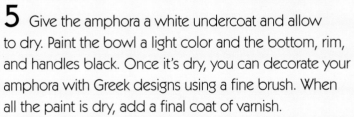

**5** Give the amphora a white undercoat and allow to dry. Paint the bowl a light color and the bottom, rim, and handles black. Once it's dry, you can decorate your amphora with Greek designs using a fine brush. When all the paint is dry, add a final coat of varnish.

You won't be able to store liquids in your amphora, but it'll make a good pencil-holder!

# Decorating temples

Ancient Greek temples were beautifully designed, with wonderful architecture and brightly painted sculptures. The most famous is the Parthenon in Athens, which was built between 447 and 438 B.C. in honor of Athena, the city's patron goddess.

The Parthenon was designed by two architects named Ictinas and Callicrates, and decorated by an artist and sculptor named Pheidias. The temple was surrounded by 46 marble columns, above which were painted relief sculptures all the way around. More relief friezes ran around the top of the inside walls, and there was a gigantic golden statue of Athena. Today, the empty ruined building is still an impressive sight and is visited by millions of tourists.

## Giant statues

Pheidias's giant statue of Athena stood inside one half of the main room of the Parthenon, which was roofed over then. The statue was made of gold and ivory and stood 40 feet (12 m) tall. It was dedicated in 438 B.C., and showed how important the goddess was to the Athenians. It also showed the rest of the world how wealthy and powerful the city was. Pheidias had already completed a giant statue of Zeus for his temple at Olympia. This temple is listed as one of the Seven Wonders of the Ancient World.

The Parthenon today. It stands on the Acropolis overlooking Athens, the modern capital of Greece.

## Friezes

Pheidias and his team of stonemasons and sculptors worked for six years carving and coloring relief sculptures inside and outside the Parthenon. Large triangular pediments at each end of the temple show the birth of Athena and her contest with Poseidon to become the patron goddess of Athens.

There are 92 small square relief panels called metopes, and a sculpted frieze runs all the way around the central block of the building. In 1801, British diplomat Lord Elgin removed 56 slabs from the frieze, with other sculptures, and took them to London. They are still displayed in the British Museum, although many people believe they should be returned to Greece.

This is how a 19th-century artist thought the giant statue of Athena looked in the Parthenon.

Part of the Elgin marbles, from the Parthenon frieze, showing Athena with Hephaistos, the god of craftsmen.

# Creating drama

Every year, the people of ancient Athens held a spring festival in honor of Dionysus, their god of wine and fertility. The festival included drama competitions, and some performances were held in an open-air theater on a slope below the Acropolis.

In Camei

This 18th-century engraving shows two ancient Greek actors dressed as old men with walking sticks.

Here stone seats curved around the stage and a building called a *skene* (or "stage house"). This was originally used as a dressing room, and artists added large painted panels to the front so that it became a background setting for the play. This background might be a palace or temple, or a simple cave or farmer's hut, depending on the action of the play.

## All-male cast

Most plays had parts for only three actors, and all were played by men. Because there were often many more characters in the play, the actors had to play several roles, ranging from young women to old men. Masks and costumes made it easier for the audience to follow the characters. Heroes and heroines had special costumes. Herakles, for example, always wore a lion skin and carried

a quiver and a club. Some masks had a calm expression on one side and an angry look on the other. This allowed actors to easily show a change of mood.

## Comedies

The earliest Greek dramas were tragic plays, mainly based on myths. They usually featured great men and women and their struggle with difficult problems. Tragedies written by Aeschylus, Euripides, and Sophocles are still famous and often performed around the world. In ancient times, comedies were very popular, too. These light-hearted dramas dealt with everyday life and family squabbles. As in more serious works, the costumes and backdrops helped to set the scene.

This ancient relief sculpture shows a comic playwright named Menander (342–292 B.C.) checking masks. The figure on the right probably represents Thalia, the goddess of comedy.

# Make an actor's mask

Actors made their masks from leather, linen, or wood. The eyes, nose, and mouth were cut out, a wig was attached, and the mask was painted with a sad or happy expression. Female masks had white skin and long hair; male masks were darker. Old men had beards and were bald. An actor's mask often covered his whole head.

A few masks from the range of Greek tragedy and comedy.

## Make a comedy mask

You will need: a round balloon • a bowl big enough to hold the balloon
• wallpaper paste • tissue paper • thick string • thin fabric • black paper
• glue • newspaper • black elastic • vaseline • scissors • a craft knife
• a pencil • red lipstick • white, ready-mixed paint • poster paints

**1** Blow up a balloon bigger than your head and knot the end. Coat it with vaseline. Tear the newspaper into strips about 1 inch (2.5 cm) wide. Cut strips of thin fabric.

**2** Mix the wallpaper paste and coat the paper strips with it. Remove any lumps before sticking each strip on and cover the balloon with a first layer. Hold the balloon in place in the empty bowl. Soak the fabric strips in paste and place a second layer crosswise on top of the first. Alternate layers of paper and fabric and cover the balloon with eight layers. Finish with a layer of fabric. Allow to dry for a day or two.

22

**3** Draw a line around the balloon, then cut a deep hollow in the back. Peel away the balloon. Try on the mask and ask an adult to cut eye-holes.

**4** Put on some lipstick, fit the mask over your head, and press your lips to the inside of the mask. Draw the mouth shape on the inside and cut it out. Make a hole for the elastic on either side of the mask, just below the eyes.

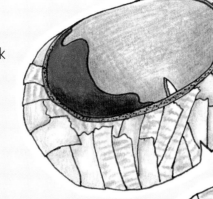

**5** Copy the features of the finished mask. Glue on crumpled-up tissue paper for the nose, thick string for the eyebrows, and rolled-up fabric for the lips. Paste a layer of paper or fabric strips over the top to cover the shapes smoothly. Allow to dry. Paint the mask white.

**6** When the mask is dry, paint the face, eyes, and lips with poster paints. To make hair, cut strips of black paper and roll them around a pencil. Glue them along the top of the head. Thread the elastic through the side holes and knot both ends.

Put on your mask and act out a Greek comedy.

# Classical sculpture

Beginning around 500 B.C., at the beginning of the Classical Age, Greek sculptors shaped the human body in a more realistic way. Artists became skilled at showing different facial expressions, and individual artists became known through the Mediterranean region.

Sculptors such as Praxiteles, who was born in Athens around 390 B.C., became famous for the expression and feeling they put into their work. Many of the best statues were carved in marble.

We know a great deal about Greek sculpture from later Roman copies. Classical Greek artists created figures in active poses rather than still ones, to show their skill and understanding of human movement. Some figures were shown taking part in the Olympic Games and other sporting events. Some were cast in bronze by the famous sculptor Myron, who made statues of victorious athletes at the games of 456 B.C.

This discus-thrower is a famous image from the ancient world. It is a Roman copy in marble of a bronze statue made by Myron. Discus-throwing was one of the five events of the original Olympic pentathlon.

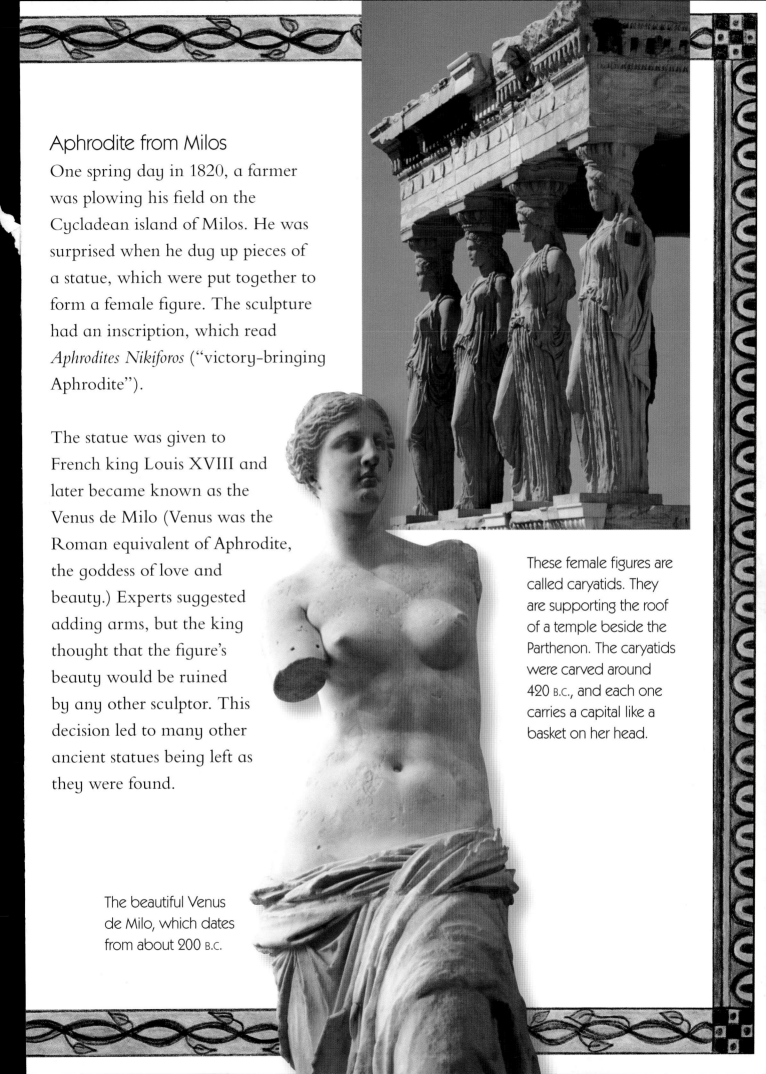

## Aphrodite from Milos

One spring day in 1820, a farmer was plowing his field on the Cycladean island of Milos. He was surprised when he dug up pieces of a statue, which were put together to form a female figure. The sculpture had an inscription, which read *Aphrodites Nikiforos* ("victory-bringing Aphrodite").

The statue was given to French king Louis XVIII and later became known as the Venus de Milo (Venus was the Roman equivalent of Aphrodite, the goddess of love and beauty.) Experts suggested adding arms, but the king thought that the figure's beauty would be ruined by any other sculptor. This decision led to many other ancient statues being left as they were found.

These female figures are called caryatids. They are supporting the roof of a temple beside the Parthenon. The caryatids were carved around 420 B.C., and each one carries a capital like a basket on her head.

The beautiful Venus de Milo, which dates from about 200 B.C.

# Writing on papyrus and parchment

The ancient Greeks developed their own system of writing around 800 B.C. They adapted the early alphabet used by the Phoenicians, a trading people from the coastal lands of the eastern Mediterranean.

The word "alphabet" comes from the Greek names of the first two letters – *alpha* (letter a) and *beta* (b). A Greek myth tells how a Phoenician prince named Cadmus brought the alphabet to Thebes, a city to the northwest of Athens. By about 650 B.C., writing was widespread in Greece, but most people did not learn to read. Myths and legends were passed on by traveling bards, or poets.

## Paper from Pergamum

Until about 300 B.C., the Greeks wrote on papyrus, made from reeds that grew beside the River Nile in Egypt. Then they began replacing papyrus with parchment, a flat, thin material made from the skins of cattle, sheep, and goats. Parchment was made mainly in the city of Pergamum (in modern Turkey), which gave the material its name. The makers scraped, smoothed,

| a | b | g | d | e | z |
|---|---|---|---|---|---|
| $A$ $\alpha$ | $B$ $\beta$ | $\Gamma$ $\gamma$ | $\Delta$ $\delta$ | $E$ $\epsilon$ | $Z$ $\zeta$ |
| e | th | i | c/k | l | m |
| $H$ $\eta$ | $\textcircled{H}$ $\theta$ | $I$ $\iota$ | $K$ $\kappa$ | $\Lambda$ $\lambda$ | $M$ $\mu$ |
| n | x | o | p | r/rh | s |
| $N$ $\gamma$ | $\Xi$ $\xi$ | $O$ $o$ | $\Pi$ $\pi$ | $P$ $\rho$ | $\Sigma$ $\sigma$ |
| t | u/y | ph | kh | ps | o |
| $T$ $\tau$ | $Y$ $\upsilon$ | $\Phi$ $\phi$ | $X$ $\chi$ | $\Psi$ $\psi$ | $\Omega$ $\omega$ |

The Greek 24-letter alphabet. The ancient Greeks used mainly capitals, and the small letters shown here gradually came into use later.

and soaked the skins in water, then dried them. Both parchment and papyrus were rolled into scrolls, and scribes wrote on them with a reed pen. Scrolls were used throughout the Mediterranean world until paper was introduced many centuries later.

The ruins of ancient Pergamum, at Bergama in modern Turkey. To the north of the city square was a great library of at least 200,000 parchment scrolls.

This marble bust of Homer is a Roman copy of a Greek original. It was designed to be mounted on a stone pillar.

## Greatest Greek poet

The most famous bard of the ancient world was Homer, who lived around 800 B.C. We know little about his life, but he may have been blind. His epic poems, including the famous *Iliad* and *Odyssey*, may have been written down after he died. The poems were recited later at religious festivals. By 300 B.C., many versions had been written down, and they are the earliest surviving works of ancient Greek literature.

# Make your own scroll

Scrolls were the books of the ancient Greeks. They pasted or stitched together sheets of parchment, and some scrolls were 33 feet (10 m) long. They wrote in columns on one side of the scroll, which they unrolled with the right hand and rolled up with the left hand at the same time. Large scrolls were hard to handle, because the reader had to unravel the whole scroll to find a particular place in the text.

Ancient writers used very little punctuation or spacing, so reading must have been very difficult!

## Make a scroll

You will need: two 12-inch (30 cm) dowel rods, 1 inch (2.5 cm) in diameter
• 4 small doorknobs • double-sided tape
• a long sheet of drawing paper • superglue
• brown and gray chalk pastels • a toothpick
• a craft knife • ink

**1** First, make the end pieces of the scroll. Glue the doorknobs to the ends of the dowel rods.

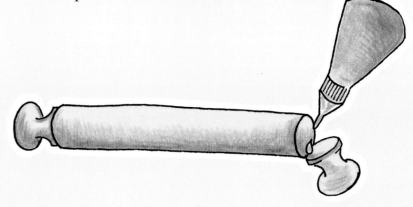

**2** To make the paper look like parchment, cover both sides with colored chalks, smudging the colors with your hand or a sponge. First, color across the paper and then from top to bottom. Use dark colors thickly, then rub in lighter colors.

**3** Cut two pieces of double-sided tape 12 inches (30 cm) long. Place the parchment in front of you with the shorter side at the top. Stick one piece of tape along the top of the paper and wrap it once around the dowel. Do the same at the bottom.

**4** Pour a little ink into a saucer. Dip a toothpick in the ink and write a message to a friend on the parchment. Use the alphabet on page 26 to help with your Greek spelling. The scroll on the right reads "GREETINGS" in ancient Greek.

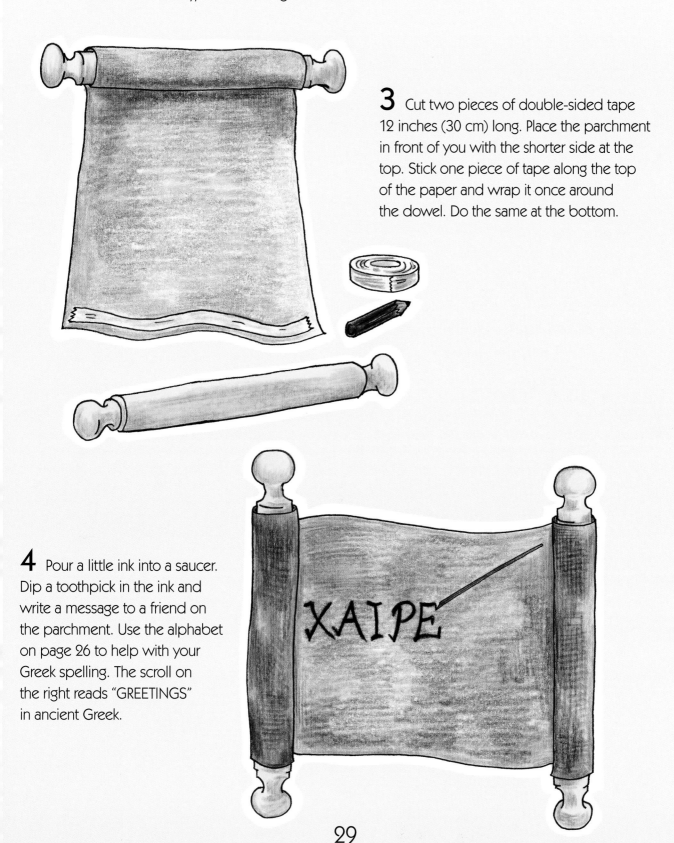

29

# Glossary

**agora** A town's marketplace in ancient Greece.

**amphora** A tall jar with two handles used for storing liquids.

**archaeologist** A person who studies the ancient past by digging up and looking at remains.

**archaic** Very old; belonging to a much earlier time.

**Attic** Relating to Attica, the region around ancient Athens.

**Bronze Age** The period after the Stone Age when people made tools of bronze metal.

**capital** The upper part of a column or pillar.

**citadel** A fortress in or near a city.

**diplomat** A person who represents a country abroad.

**drachma** A silver coin (and unit of weight) in ancient Greece.

**emery** A hard kind of rock that is used for smoothing and polishing.

**encaustic** A method of burning paint mixed with hot wax onto a material.

**equestrian** Having to do with horse riding.

**figurine** A small figure or statuette.

**fresco** A wall painting made on damp plaster.

**frieze** A band of sculpture or painting high on a wall.

**geometric patterns** Patterns made up of straight lines, circles, or squares.

**glaze** A smooth, shiny coating.

**Hellenistic period** Period in Greek history from 323 to 31 B.C., when Greek culture flourished and spread.

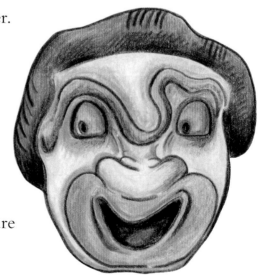

**inscription** Letters or words written or carved on a surface.

**lost wax** A method of casting bronze by melting wax in a mold and replacing it with molten metal.

**metope** A square space in a frieze.

**mint** A place where metal coins are made.

**mural** A wall painting.

**ochre** A reddish, earthy pigment (or natural color).

**papyrus** Writing material made from reed plants.

**parchment** Writing material made from prepared skins.

**pediment** The triangle-shaped upper part of the front of a classical building.

**Phoenicians** An ancient people who lived in the coastal region of present–day Lebanon or Syria.

**plaque** A flat piece of wood, metal, or stone that is decorated or inscribed.

**quiver** A case or pouch for holding arrows.

**relief** A sculpture in which figures or designs stand out from the background.

**scribe** A person who writes out documents.

**slip** A mixture of clay and water applied by potters.

**sphinx** A mythical creature with a lion's body and a woman's head.

**stonemason** A craftsman who works in stone.

**symbolic** Representing or standing for something else.

**Western civilization** The art and society of Europe and North America.

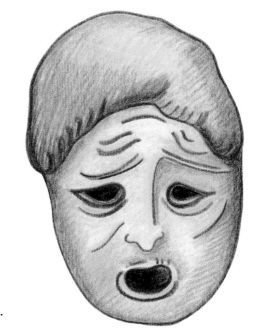

# Index